CHINESE MYTHS & LEGENDS

AS TOLD BY PHILIP ARDAGH

ILLUSTRATED BY MICHEAL FISHER

Belitha Press

MYTH OR LEGEND?

Long before people could read or write, stories were passed on by word of mouth. Every time they were told, they changed a little, with a new character added here and a twist to the plot there. From these ever-changing tales, myths and legends were born.

WHAT IS A MYTH?

A myth is a traditional story that isn't based on something that really happened and is usually about superhuman beings. Myths are made up, but they often help to explain local customs or natural phenomena.

WHAT IS A LEGEND?

A legend is very like a myth. The difference is that a legend might be based on an event that really happened, or on a person who really existed. That's not to say that the story hasn't changed over the years.

WHO ARE THE CHINESE?

Today, the Chinese people make up a quarter of the world's population. More people speak Mandarin Chinese than any other language in the world. But there are many different nationalities and groups of Chinese people, each with their own cultures and traditions.

ANCIENT PEOPLES

China has been inhabited ever since 500,000 BC. But the first real Chinese state didn't appear until 1650 BC, more than a thousand years after the birth of civilization in ancient Egypt. This state grew in the fertile valley of the Yellow River.

AN ISOLATED COUNTRY

China is a vast country that covers 9,572,900 sq km (3,696,386 sq miles). In the past it was almost completely cut off from the rest of the world. Chinese people were kept in and 'outsiders' were kept out by sea to the east and mountains and steppes to the north, south and west.

THE SECRET OF SILK

Despite being so cut off, China must have had some early trade with other countries. Chinese people were making fine silk about 1200 years BC, but the silk moth came from India, not China. Traders must have brought moths from India, and Chinese people then learned to spin thread from the cocoons.

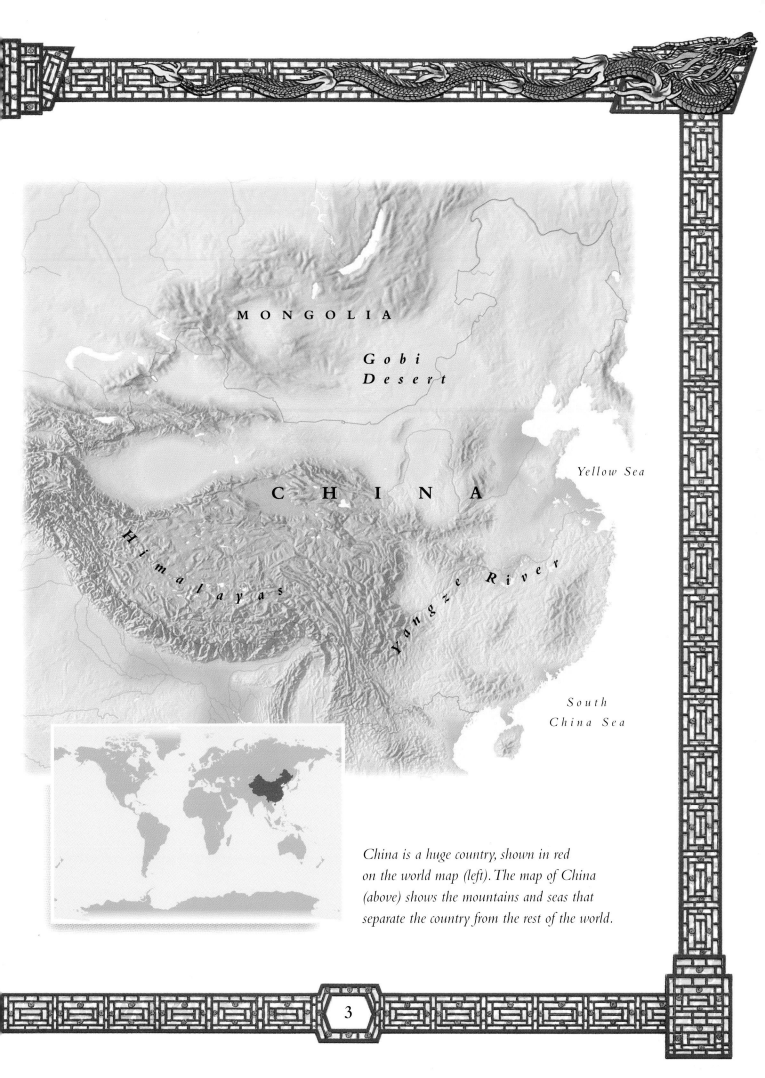

MONGOLIA

Gobi Desert

CHINA

Himalayas

Yangze River

Yellow Sea

South China Sea

China is a huge country, shown in red on the world map (left). The map of China (above) shows the mountains and seas that separate the country from the rest of the world.

TALES FROM CHINA

Chinese myths and legends are a blend of old beliefs and the stories and beliefs of three main religions: Confucianism, Taoism and Buddhism.

COMMUNIST CHINA

Today, China is a communist country. This means that all land and property is owned by the state rather than belonging to individuals. Religion plays no part in communism, but it is still important to many Chinese people.

OLD BELIEFS

The earliest Chinese religion included a belief in life after death, the worship of ancestors and the belief that the first twelve emperors were gods. A whole legendary period of history was created, with a man called Yu as the first human ruler. Historians and archaeologists are still trying to find out how much of this period is based on truth.

CONFUCIANISM

Confucianism is more a way of life – a philosophy – than a religion. It is a belief that places great importance on peace and harmony, and is based on the teachings of Confucius (551–479 BC), also known as Kong Fu Zi. He taught ideas of good government, and his followers (called Confucians) became excellent and powerful administrators.

THE WORKS OF CONFUCIUS

The lessons that Confucius taught were also interwoven with stories of the lives of the early gods. Temples were built to his honour and some people tried to declare him a god. Confucius is traditionally said to have written many books, including the famous *Yi Jing* (*The Book of Change*). Unfortunately much of his writing was destroyed in 213 BC on the orders of the first emperor of all China.

TAOISM

The influence of Confucius made people think about life and how to live. Later thinkers developed the idea of the 'oneness' of everything – that, if everything was somehow connected, it must be possible to find a way to create perfect harmony in the universe. Tao was believed to be the way. (Today Tao and Taoism would be more properly written in Western spelling as Dao and Daoism.) A book called *Tao Te Ching*, or *Dao De Jing*, which means 'the way and the power' is the centre of Taoist beliefs. It is said to have been written by a man called Lao Zi, who later became a godlike figure at the heart of Taoism.

BUDDHISM

Buddhism began in India but spread to
China sometime in the second century AD.
It became one of China's three great beliefs.
The founder of Buddhism was the Buddha
himself, born in about 560 BC. He was
originally named Gautama Sakyamuni, and
called Fo in Chinese. Buddha promised
those who followed his strict laws and gave
up worldly pleasures that they would leave
the world of life and death behind them
and enter a blissful state called Nirvana.

NOTE FROM THE AUTHOR

Myths and legends from different cultures
are told in very different ways. The purpose
of this book is to tell new versions of these
old stories, not to copy the way in which
they might have been traditionally told.
The pictures that accompany the tales are
not set in one particular period of history,
but are intended to give a flavour of life
in ancient China.

   I hope that you enjoy these stories
and that this book will make you want
to find out more about China, its peoples,
its history and its myths and legends.

*This wooden carving is just one example
of the fascinating styles of Chinese art.
It shows one of the Eight Immortals,
a group of ancient Chinese heroes.*

GOURD GIRL
AND GOURD BOY

**This is the ancient myth of Nü Wa and Fu Xi.
It tells of the foolishness of their father, a rash
act of kindness and the destruction of humankind.
It is also a tale of hope and new beginnings.**

One day a farmer was out in the fields when he heard a rumble of thunder.

'I've just about had enough of you, Thunder God!' he shouted. 'I know you send down thunder and rain just to upset me.' He cursed the god. 'Come and get me!' he yelled. 'I'm ready for you!'

The farmer hung a great big iron cage outside his house.

'Stay inside the house until I tell you to come out,' he ordered his son and daughter. 'There's some serious fighting to be done.'

The Thunder God had heard the farmer's cursing and was angry with him, so – with a mighty crash of thunder and a brilliant flash of lightning – he appeared above the farm house.

'Come down here and face me, you coward!' yelled the angry farmer. 'Don't stay up there in the clouds.'

So the Thunder God came crashing down to Earth, clutching an enormous battle axe. The farmer only had the iron fork he used in the field, but he also had the advantage. He was used to standing on the ground and on his own two feet, and was ready and waiting for this god who was shaking with rage.

With one swift movement the farmer caught him on the prongs of the fork. Before the god knew what was happening, he was flipped into the cage and the door was slammed shut.

'There!' said the farmer triumphantly. 'You can rumble and rage as much as you like now, but you can't bother me.' Soon the rain stopped and the clouds cleared. The god had been defeated.

Next morning, the farmer decided to go to market to buy some herbs.

'I think I'm going to pickle the Thunder God for all to see,' he told his son and daughter. 'You must stay well clear of the cage and don't talk to the Thunder God, whatever he might say to try to frighten you,' he insisted. 'And most importantly of all,' he added, with a stern face, 'you must not give him a drink.' With that, he set off to market feeling very proud of himself.

The farmer's son and daughter watched the god in the cage from a safe distance. He seemed harmless enough behind bars, looking sad and defeated.

As the day went on, the sun shone brightly and the children became thirsty. They had a drink. The Thunder God watched a bead of water trickle down the girl's chin.

'Please let me have some water,' he said. His voice was weak and whining, nothing like the loud bellowing of the day before. 'Please.'

'We're not allowed to talk to you,' said the girl.

'And we're certainly not allowed to give you any water,' said the boy.

'I'm sure your father didn't know today was going to be so hot,' said the Thunder God. 'On a day as hot as this, everyone should be allowed at least a sip of water – gods and humans alike.'

'Our father forbade it,' said the girl.

'For your own safety, I'd say,' said the Thunder God, clutching the bars. 'He was probably worried that I'd try to grab you if you gave me a drink.'

'Exactly,' said the boy.

'But what if I was to give you my word that I would not touch you?' said the Thunder God. 'It is so hot, and I am so thirsty locked away in this iron cage... I am a god, I will not break an oath.'

The farmer's daughter looked at the god, trapped in the iron cage in the brilliant sunshine. He was unable to move into the shade.

'Surely a few sips of water can't do any harm, can they?' she asked her brother.

'Not if he's given his word not to touch us,' said the boy.

So the two children went expressly against their father's orders and gave the Thunder God a drink. Of course, what they didn't know – and their father had neglected to tell them – was that the Thunder God drew his strength and power from water. No sooner had a drop passed his lips than he swelled in size and broke free from the iron cage as though it were made of nothing more than rice paper.

The children shrank back in terror when they realized what they'd done.

'Don't be afraid,' said the Thunder God. 'I said I would not lay a finger on you. Here is something for your kindness,' and he pulled a tooth from his mouth and threw it down before them. 'From this day on, little sister, your name is Nü Wa and yours, little brother, is Fu Xi. Now, plant the tooth and use the fruit it bears wisely,' he said and, with that, he was gone back to the heavens.

Nü Wa looked at her brother.

'What have we done?' she said. 'What will father say when he comes back and finds the Thunder God gone?'

'Perhaps if we plant the magic tooth, it will grow into something to please father on his return,' said Fu Xi.

They planted the tooth and, in next to no time, a tree sprang from the ground, bearing a single gourd that grew bigger and bigger and bigger.

'No wonder he called us Nü Wa and Fu Xi,' said his sister, because the names mean Gourd Girl and Gourd Boy. 'But what use is a huge gourd to us?' They watched in wonder as the gourd kept on growing.

Just then, it started to rain again and, by the time their father had returned from the market with his pickling herbs, there were deep puddles around the farm house.

'You realize what you've done, don't you?' said their father.

'The Thunder God has gone back to Heaven and is going to flood the Earth in revenge! Everyone will drown thanks to you!'

This was a terrible thing to say, for it was the farmer who had captured the Thunder God and angered him in the first place, not the children. And still the waters rose.

'I'm going to have to build a boat for us,' said their father. 'I pronged the Thunder God with a fork of iron, I trapped him in a cage of iron so I'll build a boat of iron.' He set to work, and the children could hear the clanging of metal above the pouring of rain.

Soon the iron boat was finished, but his children would not climb aboard. Nü Wa and Fu Xi remembered what the Thunder God had said about his magic tooth when he gave it to them – *use the fruit it bears wisely*. Hadn't he named them Gourd Girl and Gourd Boy? Why was the giant gourd so important? Because they could hollow it out and use it as a boat of their own!

So, despite the protests from their father as he clambered into his own boat, the children stepped into the giant gourd... and the flood waters rose higher and higher and higher until the two vessels finally reached the gates of Heaven.

No human had reached the gates before, so when the farmer banged hard on them with his fists and called for help, the Lord of Heaven was startled.

'What is that dreadful noise?' he demanded.

The lesser Water God nervously explained. 'The Thunder God was trapped by a human, so he asked me to flood the Earth in revenge.'

'Any higher, and your water will start to flood the heavens too,' said the Lord of Heaven angrily. 'Make the waters go!'

'Y-Yes, Lord,' said the Water God. He was so quick to please his master that he made the flood subside far too fast. One second there was water holding up the iron boat and the gourd, and the next moment there was none.

Both the iron boat and the gourd came hurtling back down to the Earth at a terrible speed. The iron boat landed with a mighty crash, killing the farmer in an instant. Luckily for Gourd Girl, Nü Wa, and Gourd Boy, Fu Xi, they had a soft landing. Their giant gourd hit the ground and bounced a few times, then the pair tumbled out on to the damp soil with nothing more than a few bruises. They were the only two people left alive on the entire Earth.

When they became adults, Nü Wa gave birth to a ball of flesh. She and Fu Xi carried it up a ladder lowered from Heaven, and cut the ball into small pieces. These they scattered in the wind and each piece that landed on the Earth became a human being. Nü Wa and Fu Xi became gods.

THE ARCHER AND THE SUNS

According to some of the earliest Chinese myths, every living thing is part of the oneness of the universe, and is made up of three things: the yin, the yang and the gi. They are held by the yin, carried by the yang and kept together by the energy of gi.

Yin is female. She is the Moon. She is water. She is the cold. She is autumn and winter. She is the shadows.

Yang is male. He is the Sun. He is dry land. He is the heat. He is spring and summer. He is the brightness.

Yin fights yang. Yang fights yin. They are locked in an evenly-matched fight to take control. The fight goes on and the natural balance is maintained. Sometimes the balance is tipped and it takes a hero to put things right. Yi the Archer was such a hero.

Beyond the horizon of the Eastern Sea, in a hot spring, there was a giant mulberry tree that reached the skies. It was called Fu Sang and was home to the ten sons of Di Jun – God of the Eastern Sky – and his goddess bride, Xi He. Their children were suns and they took turns to walk across the sky, bringing warmth and life to the Earth below. Each morning, it was the turn of one sun to make his journey. While he made his way across the sky, the other nine had to remain in the branches of Fu Sang.

Xi He ruled that there must never be more than one of her sons in the sky at any one time. And that's the way it was for a thousand years.

But the suns grew tired of the same routine, day in and day out. They wanted to do something different.

'The only time we can play together is here in the tree,' said one.

'Wouldn't it be fun to chase each other across the sky!' said another.

'Why don't we?' suggested a third.

'We can't,' said a fourth.

'Why not?' demanded a fifth.

'Because our mother forbids it,' said a sixth.

'But why does she forbid it?' wondered a seventh.

'I'm sure the humans would be pleased,' protested an eighth.

'We bring them warmth and light, and help their crops grow,' agreed a ninth.

'So let's all go out together tomorrow morning!' said the tenth, for it was night time and they were all together on the branches of Fu Sang.

The next morning, before Xi He arrived in her chariot, all ten suns jumped out of the tree and chased each other across the sky, laughing and playing.

Down below on Earth, the people were delighted.

'What a beautiful day!' they cried. 'What a glorious sight! How lucky we are to have ten suns, not just one.'

But it wasn't long before the delight turned to horror and fear. Ten times the number of suns meant ten times the brightness and ten times the heat. Crops shrivelled and died and were burned to a crisp. People were blinded by the brightness. Lakes and rivers dried up and rocks began to melt in the terrible heat. Wild animals came out of the dead, dry forests in search of food and water, and attacked people. Terrifying beasts awoke from sleep and plagued the land. The situation became desperate... but still the ten brother sons played up in the sky.

Di Jun and Xi He saw the harm their children were causing the people, and pleaded with them to return to the mighty mulberry tree. They refused. The suns had tasted freedom and they loved it!

A man called Emperor Yao prayed to the god and goddess for help. Emperor Yao was no ordinary emperor. He did not live in a palace with hundreds of servants, feast on exotic foods or wear fine silks. He preferred to live among his subjects. His home was a simple peasant's shack, his clothes were ordinary, and he ate porridge made from local wild grains. He was a humble man and a good leader, so Di Jun decided to help him.

The god sent Yi the Archer to the Emperor Yao with ten magical arrows in his quiver – one for each sun. The Emperor was delighted by Yi's arrival. The archer brought his wife Heng E (also called Chang E) with him, and the emperor made them both welcome.

Yi took up his bow, notched the first arrow, took aim and fired it at the centre of one of the suns. There was an enormous explosion, sparks flew and the sun disappeared. Something hurtled to the ground and landed nearby. Those people brave enough to venture out of doors in the heat hurried to the spot where the object had fallen. It was a three-legged raven with Yi's arrow through its heart. This was the spirit of the sun.

Yi notched a second arrow, then a third, then a fourth. Each time he extinguished a sun, a three-legged raven fell to earth, the sky became a little bit less bright, and the temperature dropped. Faster and faster, Yi destroyed the rebel suns.

Emperor Yao eyed Yi's quiver. There had been ten magical arrows in it but, now that the archer had destroyed eight suns, only two remained. Two arrows for two suns. What if Yi the Archer used both the arrows? There would be no suns left. No daylight. No warmth. No energy to grow his people's crops.

The Emperor slipped an arrow from the quiver so, when the spirit of the ninth sun fell to the ground as a raven, Yi found that he had run out of arrows and his job was done. One sun remained in the sky, which is just as it should be.

'On behalf of all my people, I thank you,' said the Emperor, and he also gave thanks to Di Jun and Xi He.

But Di Jun, God of the East and Lord of Heaven, was less pleased with Yi.

'You did as I asked, Yi,' he said. 'I do not deny that. But I cannot bear to face you every day in Heaven. Every time I see you I'll be reminded of my dead children. You and your wife, Heng E, must leave Heaven forever.'

Heng E thought that it was most unfair that she be banished to live among humans. After all, it had been her husband who had fired those arrows, not her. She noticed a change come over him. It was obvious that he was now keeping secrets and hiding things from her.

Yi had been to Mount Kunlun to visit the Queen Mother of the West. In just sixteen days he had built her the most splendid palace on Earth, with walls of the smoothest polished jade, sweet-scented timbers and a roof of glass. What Heng E didn't know was that her husband had been given a Pill of Immortality in return – one of the pills that helped the gods to live forever.

The Queen Mother of the West, a goddess, had instructed Yi the Archer carefully about the use of this pill. It should be shared – it was too powerful for one person alone – and should only be eaten after one's body had been properly prepared for it. On his return, Yi hid the pill, wrapped in a piece of silk, in the rafters of their home.

One day when Yi was away, Heng E was puzzled by a strange, magical glow coming from the rafters. She climbed up on to a beam and discovered the Pill of Immortality. Its magic was so strong that its power shone through the cloth.

She was just touching the pill with the tip of her tongue to taste it when Yi strode into the house. Some claim that Heng E then deliberately swallowed the pill. Others say she was so surprised by her husband's return that she swallowed it by mistake.

Either way, the pill – meant to be taken by two after careful planning – had now been swallowed by Heng E with no preparation at all!

The result was immediate. Heng E floated up off the rafter and out of the open door of their house and there was nothing either of them could do about it. She had no control over her body.

Up she floated – up, up, up – until she reached the Moon. There she landed and there she is still, with a hare for company. The hare is forever pounding minerals and herbs with a huge pestle and mortar.

Yi, meanwhile, built himself a palace on the one remaining sun, so that he could be up in the sky near his beloved wife. On the nights when the Moon shines brightest, he is visiting her.

So Heng E, the Moon Goddess, gives the Moon its yin – its female side. Its coldness. Its calm. Yi gives the Sun its yang – its male side. Its heat and fire. Together, they balance day and night.

THE PRINCESS
AND THE HOUND

Each Chinese year is dedicated to one of twelve animals, ranging from the monkey to the rat. This tale, based on an ancient Confucian myth, tells how the Year of the Dog got its name.

There was once a young man called Wu who was in love with a princess. He just couldn't help it. She was so beautiful that he couldn't take his eyes off her. Luckily for Wu, the Princess felt the same about him. Unluckily for Wu, he was a lowly courtier and there was no way that the Princess's father, the Emperor, would let them marry – so their love had to be secret.

One day the Emperor caught Wu looking at his daughter with love and longing in his eyes, and the old man flew into a rage.

'How dare you look upon the Princess in such a manner!' he bellowed. 'You will leave this palace never to return! Be grateful I don't chop off your head.'

The Princess wanted to say something in Wu's defence – to tell her Emperor father of their love – but she knew that this would probably make matters worse and decided to remain silent.

So Wu left the Emperor's court with a heavy heart and, with no money or possessions, went to live in the mountains. He lived a disgraced life and soon other misfits and outcasts, who had heard his sad story, came to live alongside him.

They became bandits, with Wu as their leader. With no land to grow rice and no money to buy it, a life of crime was the only answer. Wu's raiders became the terror of the foothills.

They raided farms and villages, and robbed travellers on the roads.

It didn't take long for news of this to reach the Emperor, and he ordered his army to stamp out the trouble. But Wu and his bandits knew the mountains better than anyone and disappeared behind outcrops, down gullies, or into caves hidden from view with branches.

Stories soon spread that Wu and his men could turn to mist and drift away on the wind at the first sign of trouble. This angered the Emperor even more.

'Let it be known that whoever brings me the head of Wu will not only be awarded lands containing ten thousand families, but also the hand of my beautiful daughter, the Princess, in marriage,' he declared to the Captain of the Guard.

The proclamation soon spread around the kingdom. Meanwhile, the Princess stayed in her room, refusing to eat and drink for three days, and talking to no one. She became sickly and pale.

'What is wrong, daughter?' asked her father at her bedside. Of course, he did not know of his daughter's love for the man he wanted dead.

She said nothing. There was a faraway look in her beautiful eyes.

A week later, the Emperor was sitting in a pagoda, the Princess at his feet, when a servant hurried to them with incredible news.

'Lord and master,' he said. 'Come quickly to the palace gates for there is something you will be pleased to see.'

Intrigued, the Emperor strode through the garden to the courtyard, his daughter hurrying a few paces behind him. There, standing in the open gateway stood a huge dog, with fur all the colours of the rainbow.

The Emperor's jaw dropped open in amazement and he was filled with happiness. It wasn't the dog's colours that pleased him, nor its enormous teeth and lolling tongue. No, what made the Emperor happy was what was caught up in the matted hair hanging beneath the beast's slavering jaws – the severed head of Wu.

The Emperor ordered Wu's head to be hung from the highest flagpole in the palace as a warning to those who dared look upon his daughter or lead raids against his people.

'Bring this honoured dog the tastiest of morsels,' the Emperor ordered. 'Have it bathed and its coat brushed until its rainbow colours gleam in their most radiant light –'

'What are you doing, Father?' asked the Princess.

'Why, I am rewarding the beast for a job well done,' he said.

'But didn't you proclaim that whoever brought you the head of Wu should have lands containing ten thousand families?'

'Yes,' agreed the Emperor, 'but what use are lands to this great beast?'

'You cannot go back on your word now, Father,' said his daughter.

'You are right, of course,' nodded the Emperor. He cleared his throat and made an announcement to all those present in the palace.

'As proclaimed, I now reward this dog for bringing me the head of Wu by bestowing upon it lands containing ten thousand families.'

There were gasps and mutterings of surprise from the courtiers.

'Aren't you forgetting something?' the Princess whispered in the old man's ear. 'You must marry me off to this slavering beast.'

'No!' cried the Emperor.

'Yes,' said the Princess. 'What good is the Emperor if he breaks his word?'

'Very well,' said the Emperor at last. 'But it will be a wedding in name only, daughter. I do not expect you to have to live with this creature as its wife.'

So the day of the wedding came. The Princess was dressed in her finest clothes and the vows were announced. At the end of the ceremony the dog, whom the Princess had named Ban Hu, gently picked her up between its teeth and tossed her on to its back. Before anyone realized what was happening, or had time to do anything about it, the dog ran from the palace with the Princess holding on to its fur for dear life.

'Stop them!' cried the Emperor. 'Stop them! If that treacherous beast harms so much as a single hair on my beautiful daughter's head…'

As his lord and master raged, the Captain of his Guard gathered together his men and they streamed out of the palace in pursuit of the enormous dog, the head of Wu still grinning from the flagpole high above them.

Soon the sky darkened and there was a mighty storm, with thunder, lightning and rain so heavy that each drop was like a blow to a man's back. The huge dog's paw prints were washed away, and the guards returned empty-handed.

'She is gone!' the Emperor wailed. 'Eaten, no doubt, by that multi-coloured hound.' And then he proclaimed that there would be twelve months of official mourning, when all those in the empire would grieve at the loss of his only daughter. 'It shall be called the Year of the Dog,' he declared.

The years passed, and the Emperor lay dying, when in walked his beloved daughter, the Princess. Looking up from his death bed, he wept for joy.

'I thought you were dead,' he said.

'No,' said the Princess. 'I have lived the years with Ban Hu, across the mountains. He is dead now, but we had twelve children who have a present for their grandfather.' She produced some sticks of liquorice and put one in his mouth.

The Emperor chewed on the stick and the effect was magical. The years fell from him and he was young again. He threw his arms around his daughter.

'Tell me about your husband,' he pleaded.

'Very well,' smiled the Princess. 'You see, Father, the hound and Wu were one and the same,' she said. 'I have always loved Wu. When you put out a reward for his head, I sent my spirit body to the mountains to find him.'

'That was why you were so pale, with that faraway look in your eyes!' cried the Emperor with sudden understanding. 'Your spirit was off on a long journey!'

'Yes,' said the Princess. 'And I found my beloved Wu where, with the help of my spirit body he took on the form of the ancient dog god, Ban Hu... The rest you know.'

'But was he always in the form of a dog?' gasped the Emperor.

'No,' said the Princess. 'Sometimes he became the headless Wu.'

'But that is terrible!' said the Emperor.

'No,' said the Princess. 'I loved him however he looked. Together, we found nothing but happiness.'

'And that is what you bring me, daughter,' said the Emperor. 'I misjudged Wu and I am sorry. Welcome home.'

And that is the tale of the Emperor, the Princess and Wu the lowly courtier who fairly won her hand in marriage at a great price – that of his own head.

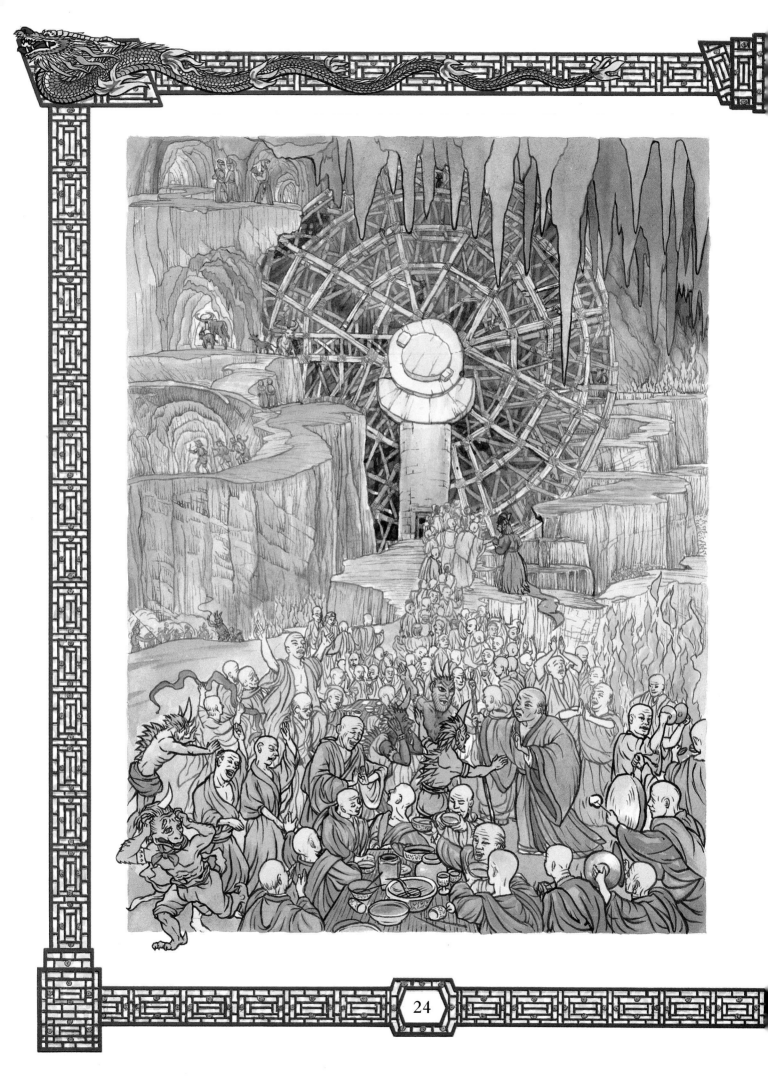

JOURNEY INTO THE UNDERWORLD

There is an ancient Chinese belief that, after death, a person's soul is judged and then placed in a new body. The identity of your new body depends on what you've done in the past. Sometimes, not everything goes as expected.

There was once a Buddhist monk who would not lie in bed at night and close his eyes. While other men and women slept, he sat bolt upright in a coffin, wide awake.

This monk did not seem to need sleep, and others soon spotted that there was something special about him.

'He must truly know the ways of enlightenment,' said one.

'The gods must have great plans for him,' agreed another.

When, years later, the monk died, he was laid out in the coffin he'd spent his nights in. He looked very peaceful and as though he was enjoying sleep for the first time.

People came to see the body of this strange holy man, and it soon became obvious that there was something unusual about his body too. When ordinary people die, their bodies begin to decay so their souls go down to the Underworld for judgement without them. This monk's body did not decay, and when he went to the Underworld, he took his body with him.

The Chinese Underworld was a series of courts where the souls of the dead were judged, punishments given out, and their next lives determined. When a soul reached the Underworld, it was taken to a court where it was weighed.

If the soul was heavy – weighed down with guilt at all the bad things it had done in life – it was passed on to another court to be judged.

Which court this was depended on the sins and crimes committed by the soul. There were different courts for different types of crimes, including greed, murder, cannibalism, lying, trading in slaves, even failing to honour your mother and father. The Buddhist monk did not visit these courts, but walked straight past them.

There was a wide range of different punishments too. Some souls were thrown to wild beasts, some were nailed to beds, some were tossed into the flames. Each court sent its victims to a different hell.

The monk was careful to avoid these too.

When the punishment was at an end, the souls reached the tenth and final court. This was where the decision was made on the new life a soul would have when passing to the Wheel of Transmigration. It was a matter of fitting old souls into new bodies, and choosing bodies that the souls deserved.

Good souls, which had been weighed and found light enough in the first court of the Underworld, passed straight to the Wheel of Transmigration. They were reincarnated as aristocrats. Souls who had been less good were sent back to Earth in the bodies of beggars or animals – but would always have a chance to better themselves the next time they died and were reborn.

As the monk stood watching the souls depart in their new bodies, one called to him as she passed through the gates of the Underworld.

'I remember you!' she called. 'Your mother's soul is still in terrible torment.'

The monk was horrified. All the while he'd imagined his mother had been born again and was living happily on Earth in some new body... Now he'd found out that her soul was still down there, somewhere, being tortured.

He hurried to the gates to find out more from the soul before she left. Just outside the gates stood the Lady Meng. She was handing each departing soul a cup of the Potion of Forgetting, called Mi Hun Tang. Once they had drunk the potion, the souls would remember nothing.

This was why no one could remember their time in the Underworld or their previous lives. What they did remember, though, was the pain. Without the memory of pain, punishment would have been pointless.

The monk was too late. The soul who had called out to him had already drunk from the cup. She remembered nothing. There was no point in asking her where she had seen his mother's tortured soul.

Like the Chinese government in the upper world of Earth, and the gods above them in Heaven, the Underworld was run by many officials. Every department of each court had hordes of them. Some recorded the weight of the souls, some recorded the sins committed, some recorded the punishments given, some recorded when the sentences were at an end, and so on and so on.

All the monk knew was that his mother had always been very good as far as he was concerned. She'd been kind to everyone. He couldn't imagine that anything she had done was very bad, and he wanted to plead for her release. The only problem was, to whom should he plead? Which court? Which official? No one seemed interested, and soon his pleas turned to demands.

Because he still had his body, the dead monk could be much more of a nuisance than an ordinary soul awaiting judgement. He could go from place to place, trying to find out more information about his mother and demanding that she be set free.

Time after time, he was met with the same official reply.

'The punishments that souls receive are for their past sins. Such punishments are drafted in Heaven and carried out in the Underworld. No one has the power to stop them.'

'My mother will be the exception!' the monk insisted. He wasn't about to give up. He went from court to court, slamming doors behind him and making as much noise as possible.

'If they're going to be difficult about this, *I'm* going to be difficult!' he declared.

He visited each of the many hells and their jailers, demanding to know if his mother's soul was being punished there. Some jailers would turn him away. Others were more helpful, feeling sorry for the monk, and they would call out his mother's name above the wails of torment and despair. Still he couldn't find her.

The search went on. His mother had looked after him in life, so it seemed only right that he should try to help her soul in death... if he could find her. It wasn't long before just about every official in all the courts, and every jailer in all the different hells knew the monk and dreaded his visits.

In desperation, he decided to hold a banquet for the souls of all the other dead monks in the Underworld, while they were waiting to be given their new bodies and to pass on to the Wheel of Transmigration.

Many of them had known this devoted Buddhist monk in life – the monk who never slept, but sat bolt upright in a coffin – and many had heard of his search for his mother's soul in the Underworld. They came in great numbers and made a great deal of noise.

It was chaos! The Underworld had never heard... never *seen* anything like it. The officials needed order to do their jobs; they needed peace and quiet, and that was something they'd had little of since the monk had begun searching for his mother's soul.

Enough was enough. The monk had won! The officials agreed to release his mother's soul sooner than planned, even if it was only in the body of a dog. At least it would get her back in the upper world and stop this soul – still with a body – from making such a fuss.

Some say that it was the Buddha himself who freed the woman's soul from the Underworld because he was so impressed by the monk's devotion to her. Whatever the reason, the monk had succeeded.

'Now, what about me?' said the monk. 'In life I needed no sleep. In death, my body has not decayed. Here in the Underworld, you have done my bidding. What do you have planned for me?'

He felt sure that he would go to the tenth court and the Wheel of Transmigration and return to Earth as a higher being. He was wrong.

The gods had decided that, because he seemed so at home among the dead souls, he should stay there with them. They named him Di Zang Wang, which means King of the Earth's Womb, and made him Lord of the Underworld. The many hells he had been so desperate to save his mother from were now part of his kingdom. Suddenly, his years of sitting in the coffin made sense. We may not always get what we expect, but sometimes we are given what we deserve.

The newly-named Di Zang Wang was given a retinue to help him in his task. They included the powerful and impressive Yan Wang, God of the Dead and judge of the first court of the Underworld, and two extraordinary demon jailers – one with the head of an ox, the other with the head of a horse.

THE RICE ROAD

This Taoist myth shows the great gulf between the rich and the poor, and how an honest magistrate was helped by one of the Eight Immortals to humble a greedy man.

The merchant and farmer Kuang Zi Lian was rich – very rich – and he loved to show off his wealth by having the biggest and best of everything. He owned thousands of fields, his clothes were made of the most exquisite and expensive silks and his enormous home was crammed full of priceless treasures.

For his birthday, he planned the most spectacular banquet that his neighbours had ever seen, and preparations were well underway. The dirt road to his home was bumpy and full of stones, so Kuang Zi Lian ordered a team of servants to clear them from the road. This was back-breaking work, and the servants carried the stones away by the basketload.

When this was done, Kuang Zi Lian went to inspect the work and found that the road was now pitted with pot holes where the stones had been.

'Have the holes filled, and a red carpet laid on top, leading under the gatehouse, through my gardens and up to the front door,' he ordered.

'What shall they fill the holes with?' asked his secretary.

'Rice!' said Kuang Zi Lian, his face breaking into a smile. 'And don't just fill the holes. I want a thick layer of rice under the carpet so that it's the smoothest of all walks for my guests!'

Now in China at that time the poor ate nothing but rice, and the very poor were lucky to eat even that. To use this food in such a way was a terrible waste, but Kuang Zi Lian saw this as another way to show just how rich and important he was. Anyone could *eat* rice. Only he was rich and powerful enough to make a road out of it.

News of this waste – at a time when people were starving – reached the magistrate in the nearby town. His name was Zhao Shen Xiao and he was a good and honest man, but there was nothing he could do about the rice road. Kuang Zi Lian could use his riches as he pleased. But Zhao Shen Xiao was saddened, and thought of all the hungry people in the towns and villages.

News of Kuang Zi Lian's forthcoming banquet had reached the local beggars and they made their way to his gatehouse with their begging bowls. They knew that there was rice beneath the carpet, but they did not dare take any, for they knew it was not theirs to take.

They dared not step through the gatehouse and into the gardens either, because they were under the watchful eye of the private guards. These guards had been given strict instructions by Kuang Zi Lian on how to treat unwanted visitors – and that was to treat them badly.

On the day of the banquet itself, however, one beggar could be found within the house. He walked among the armies of servants who were rushing here and there, finishing off the last-minute preparations. Delicious smells wafted from the kitchen, porcelain bowls glistened on row upon row of finely lacquered tables, statues were given a last-minute polish and the carpet on the rice road was given a final dusting.

The beggar walked into the kitchen and held out his bowl.

'Could you spare any leftovers?' he begged. 'My wife and children have not eaten for days.'

But the cooks did not dare give him any food, in case news of it reached Kuang Zi Lian.

At that moment, two guards entered and caught the beggar.

One wrenched the empty begging bowl from his hands, while the other grabbed him by the scruff of the neck and threw him down the outside steps to the ground. The beggar managed to lift a handful of rice from under the carpet before getting to his feet. His nose was bleeding from the fall.

The first guard grabbed his wrist and tightened his grip. 'Put that back,' he ordered.

The beggar let the rice trickle from his fingers. 'How can your master miss a handful of rice for my starving children when he has a whole road of it?' he pleaded.

'Do not question us!' said the second guard and, following their master's instructions, they kicked him to the ground as a lesson to all the other beggars.

Then came the banquet. All the wealthy land owners arrived along the rice road, marvelling at a host so fabulously rich that he could choose to use rice in this way. They admired Kuang Zi Lian's magnificent gardens, house and treasures, then all sat down for the splendid feast.

What began as cries of delight from the wealthy guests soon turned to shrieks of horror – for what had been bowls of rice turned to bowls of maggots, and noodles became writhing worms. Then the bowls themselves became too hot to hold, and the hands of the guests blistered in the painful heat. Even the finest rice wine took on the taste of mud water.

The guests were horrified, but none were more horrified than the host.

'There is trickery at work here!' he screamed, leaping to his feet. 'Two of my guards reported trouble from a strange beggar. He must have cast a spell upon us. Rest assured that he shall be punished!'

The furious Kuang Zi Lian left the banquet and ordered his guards to take him to the beggar, who still lay bleeding on the ground.

A group of other beggars had crept into the gardens to try to help him.

'This is your doing!' raged Kuang Zi Lian and he kicked the poor beggar, who took one last gasp of air then died.

Some of the beggars plucked up enough courage to report the murder to the magistrate Zhao Shen Xiao. He was outraged and made his way at once along the rice road, with a police escort, to Kuang Zi Lian's house.

When he arrived, he was surprised to see that the body of the beggar was still lying there. He'd expected that Kuang Zi Lian would have ordered it to be hidden in case there was an investigation. He soon discovered why it hadn't been moved. None of the servants could lift the dead man. His body was impossibly heavy.

Zhao Shen Xiao bent down and went through the pockets of the beggar, finding a single piece of paper. He unfolded the paper, read the few words upon it, then folded it again.

'Bring me Kuang Zi Lian,' he ordered his escort.

Soon one of the richest men in the province stood before him.

'You killed this man,' said Zhao Shen Xiao. 'I have witnesses.'

'He was a thief and on my property,' sneered Kuang Zi Lian.

'Wrong,' said the magistrate. 'This was no thief or beggar. This was Li Xuan.'

There were gasps of horror and surprise from the onlookers. Li Xuan (sometimes called Tie Guai Li) was one of the Eight Immortals – one of eight ordinary human beings who had found the road to truth and enlightenment through good deeds. This man in beggar's clothes who lay dead on the ground before them was almost a god.

Kuang Zi Lian threw himself to the ground and at the mercy of the magistrate.

'I didn't know... I didn't know...' he wailed pathetically.

'Of course you didn't know,' said Zhao Shen Xiao. 'He came here to give you a test – a test which you failed. It cost Li Xuan his life.

What is to stop me taking your life in return?'

'Spare me!' sobbed Kuang Zi Lian. 'I will give away everything. Everything, starting with the rice road. Let the food be distributed to the poor. Let my riches be sold and the money be given to charity.'

'Fine words,' said Zhao Shen Xiao. 'If you do this, I will spare you your life, so long as you spend the rest of it as a road sweeper.'

'Anything!' cried Kuang Zi Lian. 'Thank you.'

Zhao Shen Xiao smiled to himself, remembering the piece of paper inside Li Xuan's pocket. It had said: 'Spare Kuang Zi Lian's life. Make him a road sweeper.' This was followed by his signature. There had been no demand that Kuang Zi Lian give away his riches. He had done that of his own free will.

When the beggars came to lift Li Xuan he was as light as a feather. And soon after they placed him in a coffin he disappeared. It takes more than that to kill one of the Eight Immortals. Li Xuan was back with the other seven, telling them the lessons he had taught that day.

THE UGLY ONE

Many people thought Kui (sometimes called Zhong Kui) was very ugly. But Kui was not only a great scholar, he also became a god. Statues to Kui stood in many homes and most of them showed him standing on a giant turtle.

There are a number of different stories about why Kui was shown on a turtle. One of these tells how he came from a very poor family and his parents sacrificed a great deal to help him with his studies. Neither of them could read or write, but they wanted the very best for their son. His success would bring honour to all the family.

'One day you might even become a government official,' said his mother, little realizing that he would reach far greater heights than this.

From an early age Kui would study until it was too dark to read and then be up at first light, ready to start a new day of study. He had a thirst for knowledge.

He took local exams, then city exams, passing every one, all the way up to the provincial exams. He did well in every exam he took, but he was never boastful and always wanted to do better. Finally, he was ready for the most important exams of all: the Imperial Examinations.

There was some stiff competition from the other candidates, but Kui had been working towards these exams all his life, so he hoped that he would have a good chance in them.

Although Kui hoped and prayed that he would do well, and he had worked so hard to do his very best, no one was more surprised than he was when he came out with top marks. He had entered the exams with some clever scholars, and he had done better than all of them.

'Because you came first, it is a tradition that the Emperor himself will give you your honours at the palace,' the examiners told him.

Kui's family were very proud of him. His mother and father had travelled to the Imperial City to be near him on this important day.

'No one could ask for a better son,' said Kui's mother, giving him a warm embrace. She loved her son dearly, and had no idea just how ugly other people thought he was.

'Indeed,' agreed his father. 'I'll never have the honour of going to the palace.'

'It is thanks to you both that I am here today,' said Kui. 'There are many times when you have needed me to work in the fields, but have left me to my studies. I can never repay you.'

'You already have,' beamed his father. 'Your success is our reward. You are about to meet the Emperor of all China. Who knows where this might lead?'

Who indeed? Kui presented himself at the palace and was taken to the steps where he would wait to be received by the Emperor.

When the Emperor appeared, Kui kowtowed before him. This was a low and respectful bow – so low, in fact, that Kui's forehead touched the cold marble floor of the palace.

'Rise,' said the Emperor.

As Kui straightened up, their eyes met for the first time. The Emperor's imperial jaw dropped in horror and amazement. He refused to believe that anyone so ugly could really be the top student in the whole empire!

'Do you mean to tell me that this... this... *person* is the cleverest?' he spluttered. 'There has been some mistake! Take him out of my sight!'

So Kui bowed low, and backed out of the palace in silence.

What could he tell his mother and father? He should, of course, have felt angry at the unfairness of it all – but, instead, he felt ashamed.

Today was supposed to have been such a magnificent one for him and his family. Now it had turned into a day of rejection and shame.

Kui felt so downhearted and hopeless that he decided to kill himself. Without a second thought, he hurled himself into the sea.

Kui may have been good at exams, but he was not so good at trying to take his own life. There was a mighty splash and he landed on the head of a passing turtle, called Ao.

Perhaps gods were already at work. Or perhaps it really was simply a piece of good fortune for the scholar.

Startled, the turtle looked up and saw a man who wouldn't have looked out of place among his turtle friends. He decided, therefore, to steer this strange being to safety, which was extremely generous of him because Kui's clumsiness had given the poor creature a splitting headache.

The giant turtle soared out of the water and, because he was no ordinary sea creature, he continued to rise, carrying Kui higher and higher into the air. The startled expression on the scholar's face made him look even more extraordinary as he was carried all the way to Heaven.

There, Kui became God of Examinations. He was one of two assistant gods to the God of Literature, Wen Chang. Although he was only Wen Chang's assistant, Kui was far more popular than the God of Literature. Shrines to Kui appeared in most houses where members of the family were about to sit an exam.

Wen Chang may have been a more important god in the scheme of things, and was certainly better-looking with his neatly-trimmed moustache, but it was Kui who chose which candidates received top marks – so no wonder people wanted to please him.

The other assistant to Wen Chang was a god called Red Jacket. Red Jacket's role was to help some students who hadn't worked quite so hard as the others – ones who could never hope to get the higher marks, but who certainly didn't want to fail. But he only helped some of them because he, too, was a little lazy! In contrast, Kui would help every deserving candidate who prayed to him.

And what became of Ao, the giant turtle who had saved Kui's life? He was not forgotten. A likeness of his head was carved into the steps of the palace and all candidates receiving honours from the Emperor had to stand on it. The Emperor would then announce:

'May you alone stand upon the head of Ao.'

As God of Literature, Wen Chang sometimes helped students too. Once a clever candidate came home after an examination, convinced that he could have done better.

'I'm going to fail!' he groaned. 'After months – years – of work I know I could have done better… If only I could sit down and retake the exam.' And he prayed to Wen Chang. Nothing happened, and the boy went to bed depressed. He drifted off to sleep and the God of Literature appeared to him in a dream.

The images were so clear and the colours were so vivid it was as if the god was really there… as if the boy wasn't asleep at all. Wen Chang opened a stove and began to feed the flames with the essays from that morning's exam. The boy could see his own work among them.

When the papers had burnt away, Wen Chang put his hand in the stove and crumbled the ashes together. He then pulled out an essay made up of the best parts of all the burnt essays. He handed this to the boy who read it and, thinking it brilliant, read it again, memorizing it word by word.

The next morning, the student woke to hear his best friend banging on the door.

'What is it?' he asked.

'You're not going to believe this,' said his friend.

'What?'

'Bad news,' said his friend.

'What?' repeated the student impatiently.

'We're going to have to sit yesterday's exam all over again!'

'Why?' asked the puzzled student.

'Because the place where they were storing the papers was burned to the ground!' his friend explained.

The boy couldn't believe it. This wasn't *bad* news. It was quite the opposite in fact. News couldn't get much better than this! His friend couldn't understand why he was grinning from ear to ear.

They retook the exam, and the boy wrote the essay Wen Chang had given him in his dream. His prayers had been answered. He passed with his best mark ever.

Kui, Red Jacket and their master Wen Chang all live in Heaven in the constellation we know as the Great Bear. They still help students, and Kui's story is a good reminder that looks most definitely aren't everything.

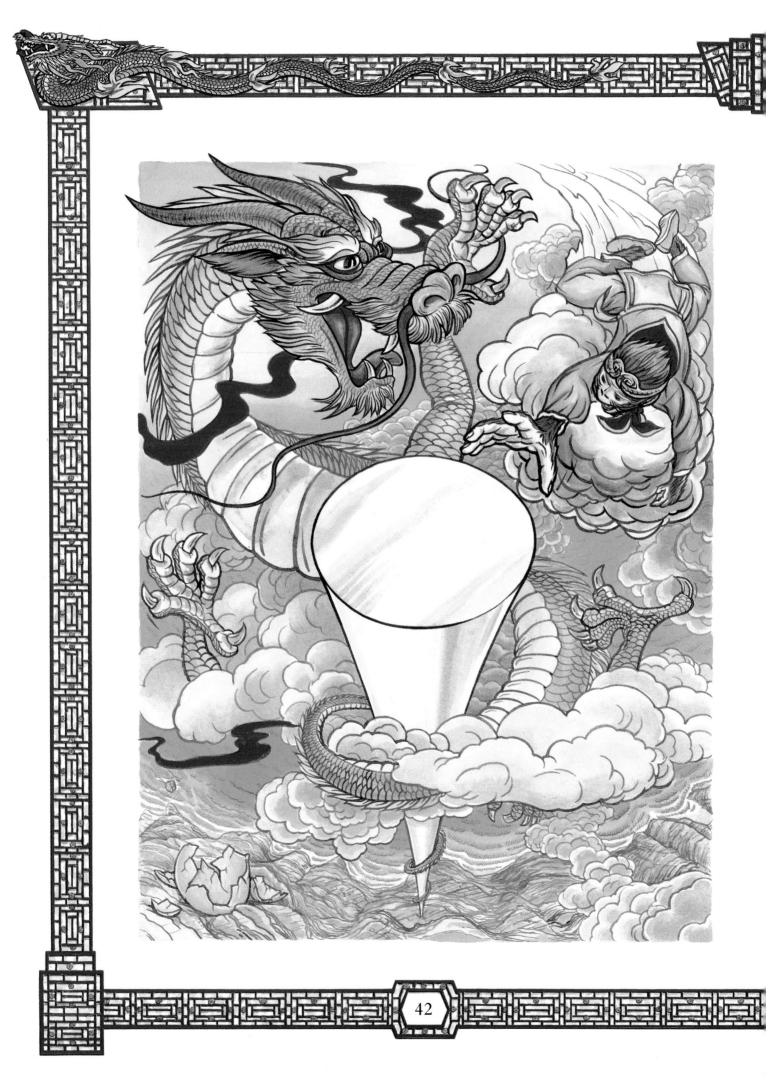

THE ADVENTURES OF MONKEY

More than a thousand years ago, a Chinese Buddhist monk called Xuan Zang (also known as Tripitaka) travelled to India to gather copies of Buddhist scriptures. His journey became a legend in which he travelled with someone called Monkey. Who was this mysterious being?

There had been a great stone egg resting on the slopes of Aolai Mountain on the shores of the Eastern Sea since the world began. It had been put there by the giant Pan Gu himself. Pan Gu was the first living being. His eyes became the sun and moon, his breath became the wind, and his voice thunder. His blood became the flowing rivers, his veins were the many roads and pathways. His fleas became the human race.

One day, the stone egg hatched and out jumped Monkey. He looked like an ordinary monkey and went to live in the mountains among the other monkeys. But they soon realized that he was not really like them. All monkeys are cunning, but he was the most cunning of them all. They made him their king.

Monkey was pleased to be king, and he ruled for many years. But after a few hundred years – some say one hundred, others say three hundred – Monkey realized that he would die one day, and he wondered what his subjects would do without him in charge.

He had heard stories of the Buddha, and had learned that those who were truly enlightened and followed him were supposed to be able to live forever.

'If that works for humans, it should work for me!' said Monkey, and off he went to the world of humans to find himself a teacher – a master – to show him the way to immortality.

Monkey was a good student and a quick learner. By the end of his years of training in the ways of enlightenment, he could turn himself into anything he wanted to be, or fly through the skies on a cloud. He had also found the way to live forever.

Monkey returned home happy, only to find that the other monkeys were living in fear of a dreadful monster that had been terrorizing them while he had been gone. With his new powers, Monkey was able to defeat the beast and its followers, but afterwards he realized that this would have been a much easier task if he had had a special weapon.

He knew that the Dragon King of the Eastern Sea, where he had been born, guarded a pillar of iron. In the blinking of an eye it could become a tiny needle, a column reaching from the ground to Heaven, or a fighting staff. This would make a very useful weapon indeed... so Monkey stole it from the dragon, and kept it behind his ear for emergencies. He also had a magic cudgel – a great big club – that he liked to wave above his head to taunt his enemies.

With his new-found knowledge and strength, Monkey settled down to a peaceful life among his fellow monkeys. But one day, in the middle of a feast, two guards from the Underworld appeared. It was their job to lead souls to the Underworld to die at their allotted time.

'We have come for you,' they said to Monkey.

'But I'm supposed to live forever!' he protested.

Monkey was so angry that he hit both of the guards over the head then flew off to the Underworld in a terrible rage. He burst into the courts of Hell and demanded to see the Register of the Dead.

When he looked in the book, Monkey discovered that the guards had been telling the truth – he was indeed due to die that day. Shaking with anger, he took a brush and crossed out his name.

The Lord of the Underworld complained to the chief god, the Jade Emperor. The Jade Emperor had already had complaints about Monkey from the Dragon King, so he decided he must act quickly.

He knew that there was one thing Monkey wanted more than anything else. He wanted to be important. So the Jade Emperor offered Monkey a job with an important-sounding title: Keeper of the Heavenly Horse.

Monkey was very proud to accept, unaware that the Emperor simply wanted him up in Heaven so he could keep an eye on him. It soon dawned on Monkey, though, just how unimportant this job was. He was about to get up to some of his old mischief-making when he was offered an even more important-sounding role: Great Sage, Equal of Heaven. But again, this was an important-sounding unimportant job.

Finally Monkey was given a job that really was important. He was made Guardian of the Garden of Immortal Peaches. This wasn't a very good idea because, as their name suggests, these were no ordinary peaches. This was the fruit eaten by the Immortals to make sure that they would live forever. It took six thousand years for the crop of peaches to ripen. After these had been eaten, it would be another six thousand years before the next crop was ripe enough to eat.

'What harm can I do eating just one?' thought Monkey. It was so delicious that he quickly followed it with another and another and another. By the time a group of maiden spirits arrived to pick the fruit for the Immortals' feast, Monkey was fast asleep in one of the trees, snoring loudly.

It didn't take much for the spirits to guess what had happened, with so many peaches missing and Monkey up a tree with peach stones scattered on the ground below him. They hurried off to tell Xiwangmu, the Queen of the West, who owned the garden.

When the Queen heard the news, she was so angry that she decided not to invite Monkey to the feast with the other Immortals.

When Monkey heard this, he decided to eat most of the remaining peaches, as well as the wine he'd found in some gourds.

What he didn't realise was that this was the Elixir of Immortality, that Lao Zi – the founder of Taoism – was bringing to the feast. Monkey drank every last drop. Then he fell into an even deeper sleep.

When Monkey woke up later he was filled with a terrible guilt. He hurried back to his mountain home among the monkeys and hoped that the gods wouldn't find him.

When the Jade Emperor was told of the unforgivable things Monkey had done this time, his patience ran out. He sent an army of one hundred thousand heavenly soldiers to capture him. There was battle after battle, and when Monkey was finally caught and taken to the Jade Emperor there was no way that he could be sentenced to death. Monkey had eaten so many of the peaches and drunk so much of the elixir that he would live forever.

Instead, the Jade Emperor ordered that Monkey be put into Lao Zi's furnace, where he would be melted into different parts so, even though he would still be alive, he wouldn't be able to do any harm. But when, after forty-nine days, the doors to the furnace were opened, Monkey jumped out, rubbing his eyes.

'Smoky in there!' he commented, then dashed off with a chattering monkey's laugh.

The Jade Emperor was desperate. Was there no way to calm this troublemaker? He decided to ask the Buddha for help. Buddha picked up Monkey by the scruff of the neck and placed him in his hand.

'If you can jump out of my hand, Monkey, I will make you the ruler of Heaven in the place of the Jade Emperor,' he said. 'If you can't, you must return to Earth and work hard to earn your right to live forever.'

'Fair enough,' grinned Monkey. He leaped high in the air and, after a long, long fall, landed at the foot of five huge pillars that were so tall that the tops disappeared into the mist far, far above.

'That was easy!' he laughed and, plucking out one of his hairs and using it as a brush, he wrote his name at the bottom of the middle pillar.

When he found Buddha looking down at him, Monkey claimed his right to rule Heaven.

'But you never left my hand,' said Buddha.

'Oh yes I did,' said Monkey indignantly, and told Buddha about the pillars and writing his name.

It was Buddha's turn to smile.

'Those five pillars were my five fingers,' he said. 'Look.'

And, when he looked closely, Monkey could make out the word 'MONKEY' at the base of Buddha's middle finger. He sighed. He had been defeated at last.

But Monkey's adventures had only just begun. As assistant to the Buddhist monk Xuan Zang, he soon became the hero of a series of amazing escapades. These are told in a famous sixteenth-century book called *Journey to the West*, and they are still some of the most popular stories in China.

INDEX

First published in the UK in 1999 by
Belitha Press Ltd
London House, Great Eastern Wharf,
Parkgate Road, London SW11 4NQ

Copyright © Belitha Press 1999
Text copyright © Philip Ardagh 1999
Illustrations copyright © Belitha Press 1999

Philip Ardagh asserts his moral right to
be identified as the author of this work.

All rights reserved. No part of this book
may be reproduced or utilized in any form
or by any means, electronic or mechanical,
including photocopying, recording or by
any information storage and retrieval
system, without permission in writing from
the publisher, except by a reviewer, who
may quote brief passages in a review.

ISBN 1 85561 820 6

British Library Cataloguing in Publication
Data for this book is available from the
British Library.

Editor: Stephanie Bellwood
Designer: Jamie Asher
Consultant: Ming Wilson
Educational consultant: Liz Bassant
Series editor: Mary-Jane Wilkins

Printed in China